Editor
Gisela Lee, M.A.

Managing Editor
Karen J. Goldfluss, M.S. Ed.

Editor-in-Chief
Sharon Coan, M.S. Ed.

Illustrator
Ken Tunell

Cover Artist
Barb Lorseyedi

Art Coordinator
Kevin Barnes

Imaging
Temo Parra
Rosa C. See

Product Manager
Phil Garcia

Publishers
Rachelle Cracchiolo, M.S. Ed.
Mary Dupuy Smith, M.S. Ed.

Practice Makes Perfect

Map Skills

GRADE 3

Author
Jennifer Overend Prior, M.Ed.

Teacher Created Materials, Inc.
6421 Industry Way
Westminster, CA 92683
www.teachercreated.com
ISBN-0-7439-3728-7
©2003 Teacher Created Materials, Inc.
Made in U.S.A.

Table of Contents

Introduction

Using map skills is a great way for children to organize information around a fixed point of reference. The use of maps enables children to see and describe locations, landmarks, and geographic areas.

Using a map involves more than just identifying cardinal directions. This book focuses on the following map-related skills:

- understanding cardinal and medial directions
- using a map key or legend
- measuring distance using a map scale
- locating places and landmarks using a map grid

- following directions using a map
- map making
- identifying and labeling continents and oceans
- understanding a weather map

This book contains practice pages that are organized sequentially, so children can build their knowledge from basic skills to higher-level map skills. Following the practice lessons are six practice tests. These provide children with multiple-choice test items to help prepare them for standardized tests administered in schools. As your child completes each test, he or she should fill in the correct bubbles on the answer sheet (page 45). To correct the test pages and the practice lessons in this book, use the answer key provided on pages 46–48.

How to Make the Most of This Book

Here are some useful ideas for optimizing the practice lessons in this book:

- Set aside a specific place in your home to work on the practice pages. Keep it neat and tidy with materials on hand.
- Set up a certain time of day to work on the practice pages. This will establish consistency. An alternative is to look for times in your day or week that are less hectic and more conducive to practicing skills.
- Keep all practice sessions with your child positive and constructive. If the mood becomes tense, or you and your child are frustrated, set the book aside and look for another time to practice with your child.
- Help with instructions, if necessary. If your child is having difficulty understanding what to do or how to get started, work through the first question with him or her.
- Review the work your child has done. This serves as reinforcement and provides further practice.
- Allow your child to use whatever writing instruments he or she prefers. For example, colored pencils can add variety and pleasure to drill work.
- Pay attention to the areas in which your child has the most difficulty. Provide extra guidance and exercises in those areas. Allow your child to color the maps in the book. Maps of familiar places can help him or her to grasp difficult concepts more easily.
- Look for ways to make real-life applications to the skills being reinforced.

Consider enlisting your child's help in planning a road trip or even a trip through town. The more meaningful the experience, the more likely it is that your child will learn and retain the skills.

What Are Maps and Globes?

What is a Map?

A map is a picture of a place. It shows where things are located. For example, a map of a bedroom might show where the bed, dresser, and closet are. A map of a city often shows streets, highways, schools, and attractions or landmarks.

There are many kinds of maps, such as world maps, country maps, state and city maps, weather maps, and population maps.

What is a Globe?

A globe is a model of Earth. It is like a map, but it is round. A globe gives a better picture of how the world looks. The round part of a globe rests on a stand, and it can turn the way Earth turns. Both maps and globes give lots of information about many kinds of places.

Answer the questions and complete the sentences.

1. A map is a picture of _____.

2. What are three kinds of maps?_____

3. What are two things that might be found on a city map? _____

4. How is a globe different from a map? _____

5. A globe is a model of _____

6. What do maps and globes give us? _____

_____

Cardinal Directions

A map uses a tool to show directions. This tool is called a compass rose. The compass rose can show the directions north, south, east, and west. Some compass roses use full words for the directions. Some use the beginning letter to represent each direction. Look at the compass rose on the right.

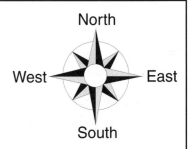

Write the direction word(s) that is missing on each compass rose below.

1.

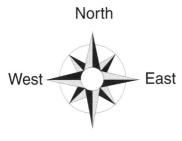

4.

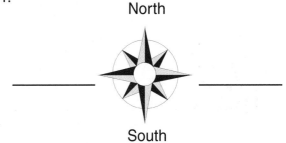

2.

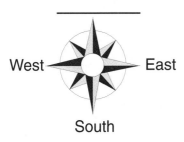

5.

3.

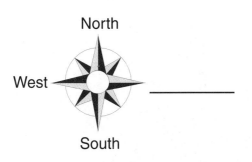

6.

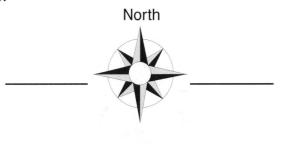

Medial Directions

Some compass roses show directions that are in between north, south, east, and west. This helps give a better idea of where something is located on a map. These medial directions are northeast, northwest, southeast, and southwest. Look at the compass rose on the right. You will notice that the directions are represented by letters.

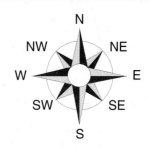

Write the direction letters that are missing on each compass rose.

1.

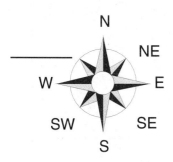

2.

4.

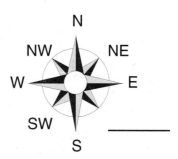

5.

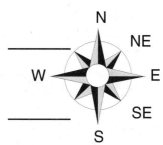

3.

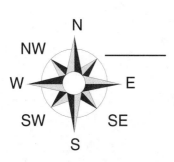

6.

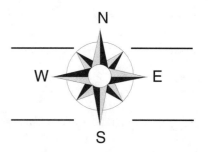

Neighborhood Directions

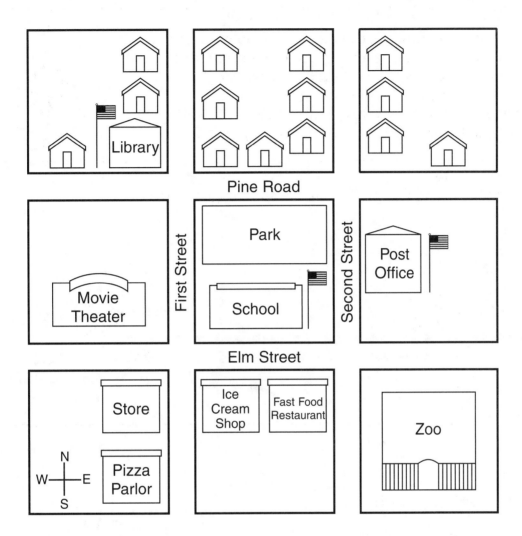

Use the map to answer the questions.

1. Which road is north of the park? _____

2. Which street is east of the school? _____

3. What shop is northeast of the pizza parlor? _____

4. What building is north of the store? _____

5. If you were at the library, in what direction would you travel to get to the post office?

    _____

6. Which two buildings are south of the school? _____

    _____

City Directions

Use the map below to answer the questions on page 9.

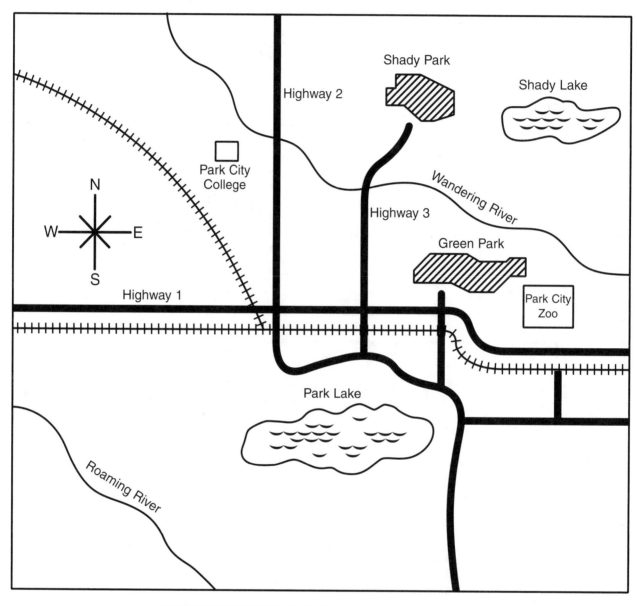

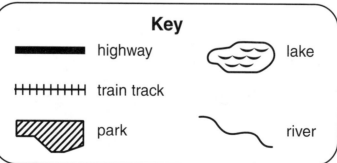

Key

▬▬▬	highway	🌊	lake
++++++++	train track	〜〜	river
▨	park		

City Directions (cont.)

Answer the questions below using the map of Park City on page 8.

1. Which park is in the northern part of the map?

_____

2. Does Highway 2 run north/south or east/west?

_____

3. Which lake is south of the train track?

_____

4. Does Roaming River run southeast or southwest?

_____

5. The Park City Zoo is in which direction from Green Park?

_____

6. Is Park City College east or west of Highway 2?

_____

7. Which two highways cross Wandering River?

_____

8. Shady Lake is which direction from Green Park? (Use medial directions.)

_____

9. Park Lake is which direction from the college? (Use medial directions.)

_____

10. If you drive east on Highway 1, which park would you pass?

_____

Using a Map Key

Maps use symbols that represent places or things. These symbols are found in the map's key.
The key is also called a legend. Look at the symbols on the map key below.

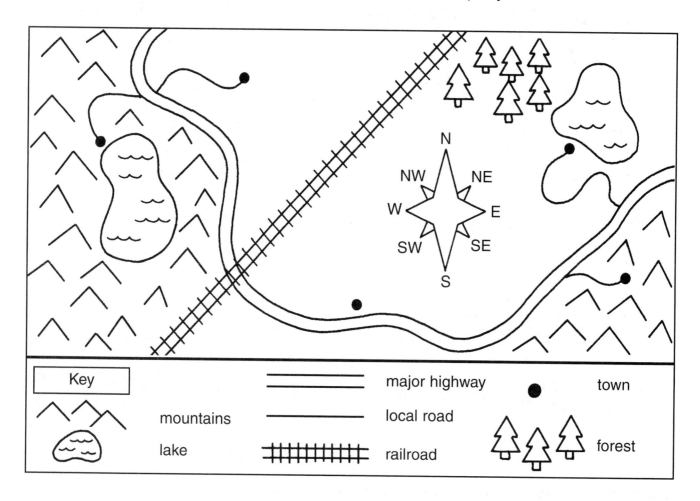

Answer true or false. If it is false, write the correct answer above the sentence.

1. _____ A railroad track runs southwest to northeast.

2. _____ Mountains cover the northern section of the map.

3. _____ A lake and a forest are in the southeast.

4. _____ All towns can be reached by the major highway.

5. _____ Two towns are by lakes, and two towns are in the mountains.

6. _____ There are no towns along the railroad track.

7. _____ There is a large forest east of the lake and west of the railroad.

8. _____ The southernmost town is next to the major highway.

Using a Map Legend

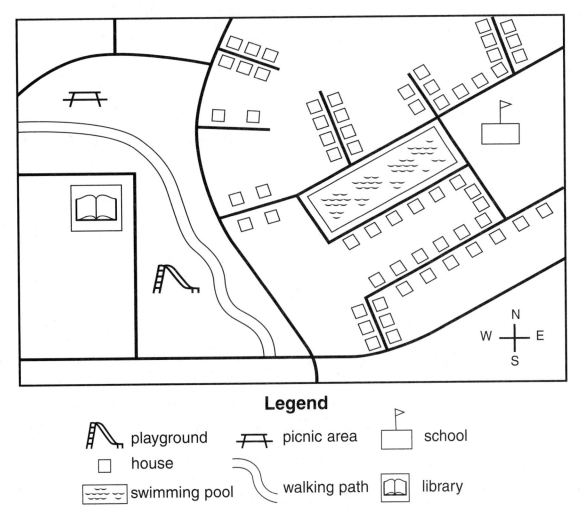

Legend

 playground   picnic area   school

   house

swimming pool   walking path   library

Use the map and legend to answer the questions.

1. What building is northeast of the swimming pool?

_____

2. The walking path passes which three areas?

_____

3. What is south of the picnic area?

_____

4. Does the walking path run southeast or northeast?

_____

5. How many houses are on the street that runs northwest from the swimming pool?

_____

6. What direction is the school from the playground? (Use medial directions.)

_____

Key to Florida

Use the map below to answer the questions on page 13.

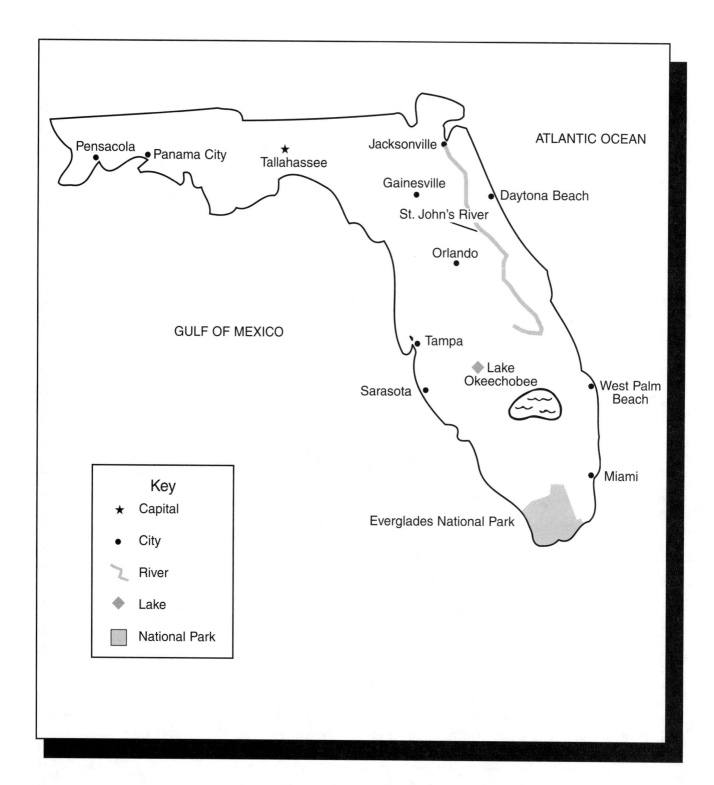

Pensacola ● Panama City ★ Tallahassee Jacksonville ●

ATLANTIC OCEAN

Gainesville ●

Daytona Beach ●

St. John's River

Orlando ●

GULF OF MEXICO

Tampa ●

Lake Okeechobee ◆

West Palm Beach ●

Sarasota ●

Miami ●

Everglades National Park

Key

★ Capital

● City

River

◆ Lake

National Park

Key to Florida *(cont.)*

Use the map of Florida on page 12 to answer the questions below.

1. What does the star represent? _____

2. What do the black dots or circles represent? _____

3. What does the diamond shape represent? _____

4. What is the name of the capital city? _____

5. What is the name of the lake? _____

6. What city is near the most northern part of the St. John's River? _____

7. What is represented by a dark, shaded area? _____

8. What body of water is east of Daytona Beach? _____

9. What body of water is north of the national park? _____

10. The Gulf of Mexico is in which direction from the capital city? _____

Create a Map

Use the directions on page 15 to draw a map below.

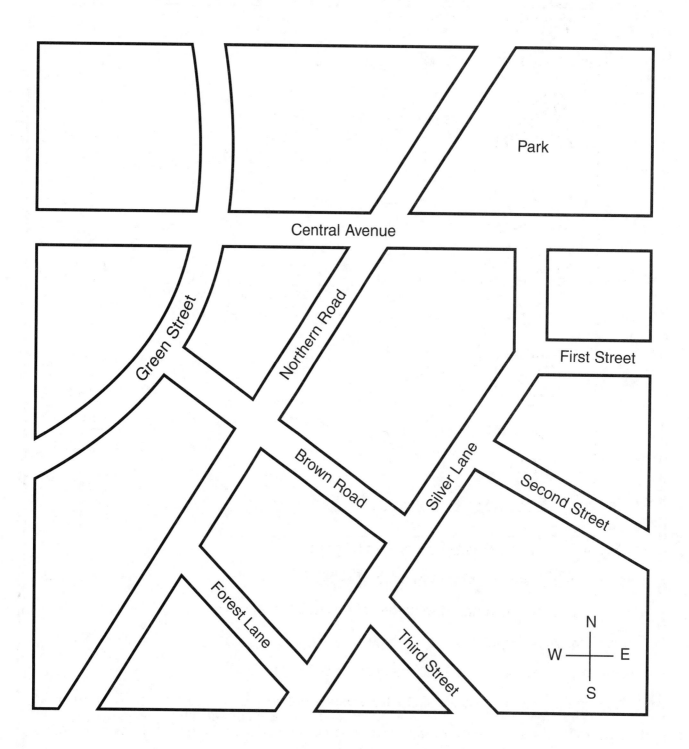

Park

Central Avenue

Green Street

Northern Road

First Street

Brown Road

Silver Lane

Second Street

Forest Lane

Third Street

N
W E
S

Create a Map (cont.)

Use the directions and symbols below to complete the map on page 14.

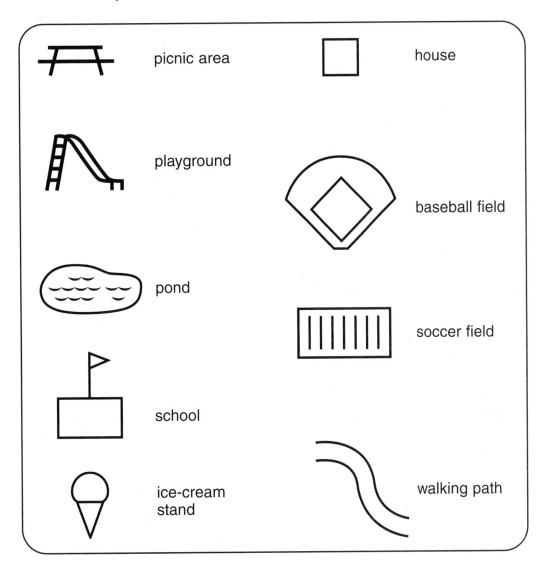

1. Draw a pond in the southwest corner of the park.

2. Draw a picnic area in the northeast corner of the park.

3. Draw a baseball field near the corner of Forest Lane and Silver Lane.

4. Draw the school on the northwest corner of Green Street and Central Avenue.

5. Draw a playground in the southeast corner of the park.

6. Draw the soccer field south of Central Avenue between Silver Lane and Northern Road.

7. Draw the ice cream stand on the northeast corner of Silver Lane and Second Street.

8. Draw three houses on both sides of First Street and Third Street.

Map of England

Use the map and legend to answer the questions on page 17.

Legend

★ capital

• city

∧ mountains

------ borderline

—— river

Map of England *(cont.)*

Use the map of England on page 16 to answer the questions.

1. What are the names of three cities shown in the southern half of England?

   _____

2. Which city on the map is closest to the Severn River?

   _____

3. If you were in Bristol, which direction would you travel to go to the mountains?

   _____

4. What do the stars represent on the map?

   _____

5. What do the dots represent on the map?

   _____

6. What is the name of the capital city of England?

   _____

7. Which direction would you travel to go from the capital city of England to Manchester? (Use medial directions.)

   _____

8. Which body of water is closest to the mountains?

   _____

9. Which river is southeast of the Severn?

   _____

10. Which river is closest to London?

   _____

Using a Map Scale

Places and objects on a map are drawn smaller than they actually are. A scale is a tool used to measure distance on a map. You can use a scale to figure out the number of miles (or kilometers) are between locations.

Look at the scale below. It gives a measurement on a map and what that means in terms of distance. On this scale, one inch on a map equals one mile in actual distance. If two cities were two inches apart on a map, they would actually be two miles apart.

Use the scale on this page to answer the questions about the map below. Use a ruler to help you. (*Hint:* If you do not have a ruler, draw the scale on the edges if a piece of paper and use it to help you measure.)

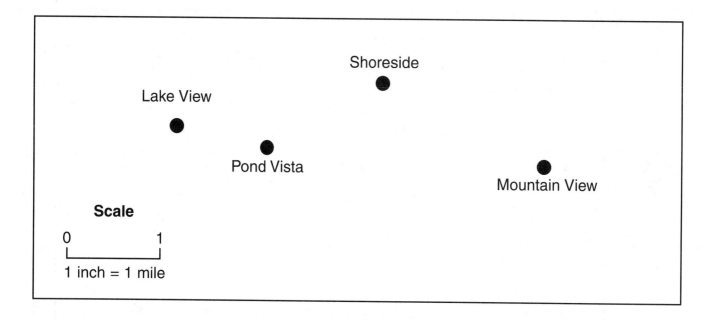

1. How many miles does one inch equal on this map? _____

2. How many inches is it from Pond Vista to Shoreside? _____

3. How many miles does that equal? _____

4. How many miles is it from Lake View to Mountain View? _____

5. How many miles is it from Lake View to Pond Vista? _____

6. How many miles is it from Pond Vista to Mountain View? _____

Using More Map Scales

The map below uses a scale to measure distance between locations. You can see that one inch on the map equals one mile. Use the scale to answer the questions about the map. (You can use a ruler or trace the scale on a slip of paper to help.)

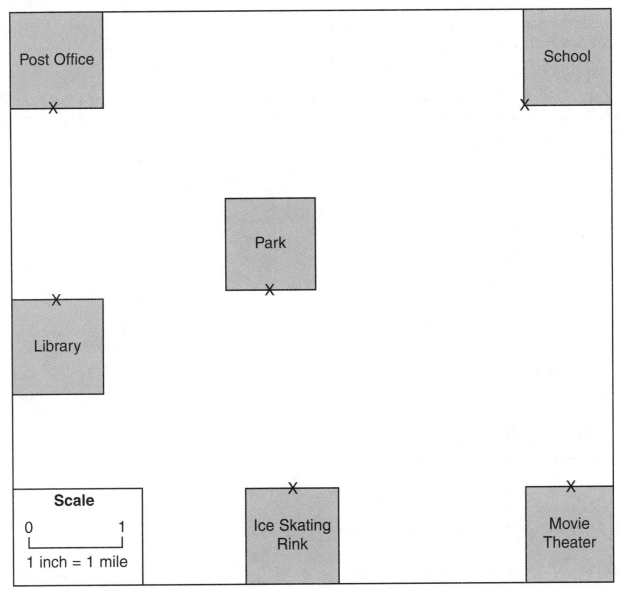

1. Measure the distance between the post office and the library. About how many miles does that equal? _____

2. Measure the distance between the park and the movie theater. About how many inches did you measure, and how many miles does that equal? _____

3. Measure the distance between the post office and the school. About how many miles does that equal? _____

4. About how many miles is it from the ice skating rink to the school? _____

5. About how many miles is it from the movie theater to the school? _____

6. If you were at the movie theater, about how many miles would you walk if you went to the park and then to the ice skating rink? _____

Alberta to Scale

Some map scales are not measured from inches to miles. Some scales show a line that represents the distance on the map and then tell the number of miles (mi) or kilometers (km). Look at the scale for the map below.

Trace the scale onto a slip of paper. Use the scale to answer the questions on page 21 about a province in Canada called Alberta.

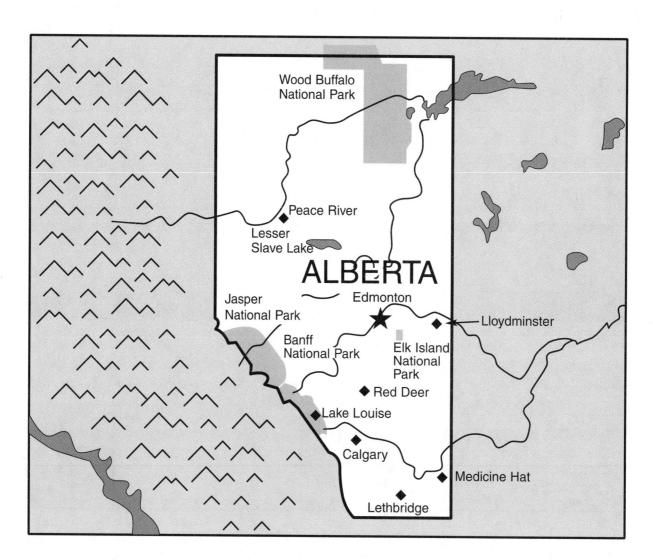

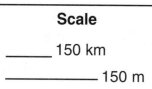

Scale

_____ 150 km

_____ 150 m

Alberta to Scale *(cont.)*

Use the map and scale on page 20 to answer the questions below. Write each answer using both types of measurements.

1. How far is it from Peace River to Calgary?

_____

2. How far is it from Red Deer to Lloydminster?

_____

3. Which is closer to Edmonton: Lethbridge or Wood Buffalo National Park?

_____

4. How far is it between Medicine Hat and Calgary?

_____

5. How far is it from Lesser Slave Lake to the northern border of Alberta?

_____

6. How far is it from Red Deer to Medicine Hat?

_____

7. Is it farther to go from Edmonton to Medicine Hat or from Peace River to Wood Buffalo National Park?

_____

8. How far is it from Lethbridge to Lloydminster?

_____

9. How many kilometers is it from Edmonton to Red Deer?

_____

10. How many miles would you travel if you started at Medicine Hat, then went to Red Deer, and then went to Lesser Slave Lake?

_____

Mileage Charts

Sometimes maps include mileage charts. These tell how many miles (or km) a person would drive from one place to another.

In the left column, find Amarillo, TX. Now, follow the row across until you reach New York, NY. You can see that if you drove from Amarillo to New York City it would be 1,704 miles.

Use the mileage chart to answer the questions on page 23.

United States Mileage Chart (in miles)

	Atlanta, GA	Boston, MA	Chicago, IL	Dallas, TX	Los Angeles, CA	Memphis, TN	Minneapolis, MN	New York, NY
Amarillo, TX	1,097	1,897	1,043	358	1,091	726	975	1,704
Denver, CO	1,398	1,949	996	781	1,059	1,040	920	1,771
Flagstaff, AZ	1,704	2,495	1,604	961	484	1,333	1,481	2,302
Miami, FL	655	1,504	1,329	1,300	2,687	997	1,723	1,308
New Orleans, LA	479	1507	912	496	1,883	390	1,214	1,311
Norfolk, VA	540	558	831	1,329	2,694	877	1,236	362
Pittsburgh, PA	687	574	452	1,204	2,426	752	857	368
Tulsa, OK	772	1,537	683	257	1,452	401	695	1,344

Mileage Charts *(cont.)*

Use the mileage chart on page 22 to answer the questions below.

1. How many miles is it from Denver to Boston?

   _____

2. How many miles is it from Tulsa to Memphis?

   _____

3. Is Flagstaff or Norfolk closer to New York?

   _____

4. Is Miami or Denver closer to Dallas?

   _____

5. Which cities on the chart have the shortest distance between them?

   _____

6. Which cities on the chart have the greatest distance between them?

   _____

7. If a person drove about 50 miles per hour, how many hours would it take to get from Tulsa to Dallas?

   _____

8. If a person drove about 50 miles per hour, how many hours would it take to get from Pittsburgh to Chicago?

   _____

9. If you were in Flagstaff, would it take longer to get to Los Angeles or Boston?

   _____

10. If you were in Minneapolis, would it take longer to get to Miami or New Orleans?

   _____

Continents and Oceans

A world map is another kind of map that is often used. It shows oceans and land masses. There are four oceans and seven continents. Use the world map below to answer the questions.

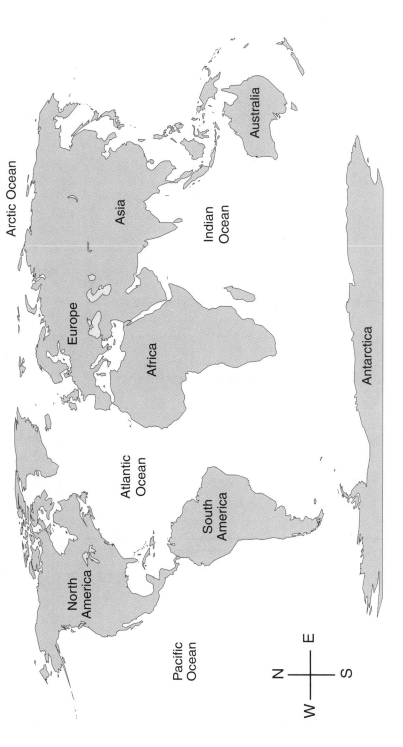

1. What is the name of the continent on which you live? _____

2. Which two oceans border Africa? _____

3. What ocean is south of Asia? _____

4. Which two continents are to the east of the Pacific Ocean? _____

5. Which ocean separates North America from Europe? _____

6. Which continent is closest to Antarctica? _____

Continents and Oceans *(cont.)*

Here is another world map. You will notice that the oceans and continents are not labeled. Write the names of the continents and oceans on the lines.

Use the list below to help you.

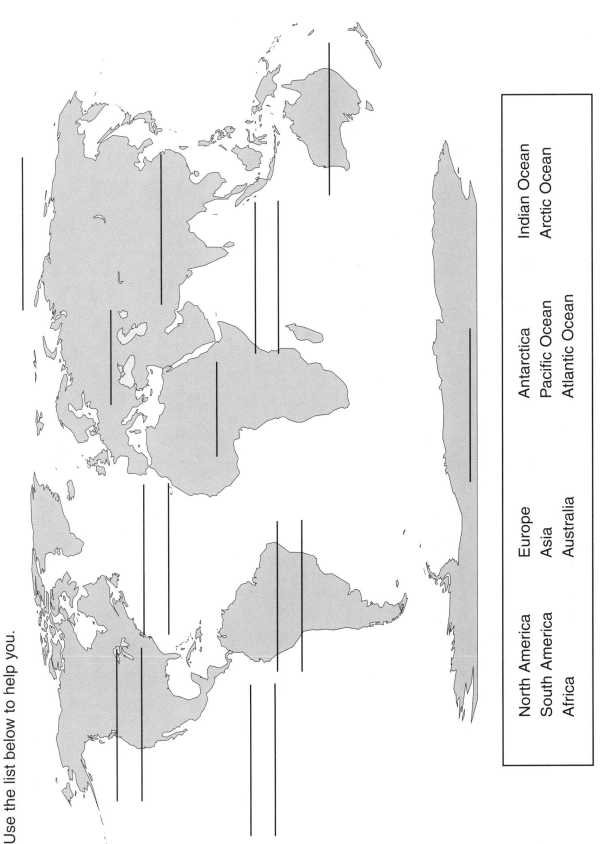

North America	Europe	Antarctica	Indian Ocean
South America	Asia	Pacific Ocean	Arctic Ocean
Africa	Australia	Atlantic Ocean	

The United States

This is a map of the United States of America. The U. S. has 50 states. Two of the states are not connected to the others. In the lower left corner of the map, you can see Alaska and Hawaii. Alaska is attached to Canada and Hawaii is a group of islands in the Pacific Ocean.

Answer the questions and follow the directions.

1. Which four states border Texas? _____

2. List three states that begin with the letter A. _____

3. Which states surround Nebraska? _____

Color each state. Try to use as many colors as you can.

Outline your state using a black crayon or marker.

Canada

This is a map of Canada. This country is divided into areas called provinces and territories. This map also shows cities and lakes. Use the map to answer the questions.

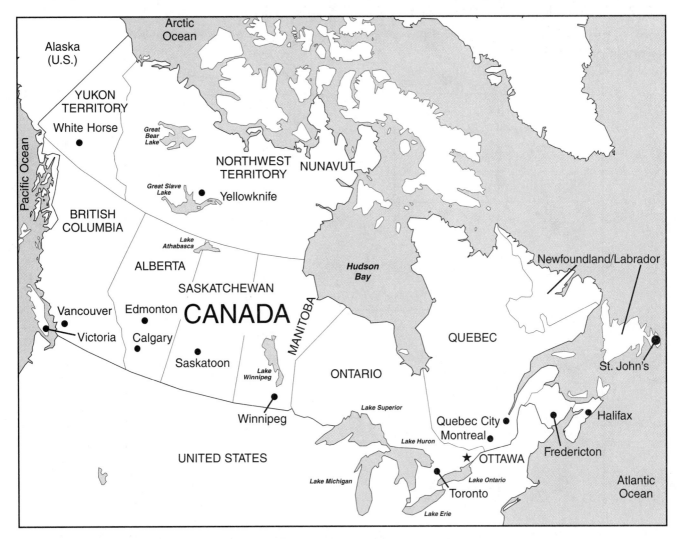

1. How many oceans border Canada? _____

2. What is the name of a city shown in Alberta? _____

3. Which provinces and territories surround the Hudson Bay?

   _____

4. What is the name of a city shown in Ontario? _____

5. Which lakes border Canada and the United States? _____

   _____

6. Which territory has two large lakes? _____

Using a Map Grid

A grid is a group of lines drawn and labeled in a special way. The vertical (up and down) columns are labeled with numbers. The horizontal (across) columns are labeled with letters. Grids are often drawn on top of maps. This helps when trying to locate unfamiliar locations.

Look at the grid below. Follow the directions to draw a map on the grid below. Use the symbols on the key.

	A	B	C	D	E
1					
2					
3					
4					

Key to Woodland Park Recreational Area

lake   mountains   camping area

river   orchard   restrooms

1. Draw a lake that covers part of 2B, 3B, 2C, and 3C.

2. Draw a river that begins in 1D and ends in the lake.

3. Draw mountains in 5A, 5B, and 5C.

4. Draw an orchard in 2D and 3D.

5. Draw camping areas in 1A, 2A, 1C, 4C, and 4D.

6. Draw a restroom in 4B.

Using More Map Grids

Notice the grid on this world map. Use the map and grid to answer the questions.

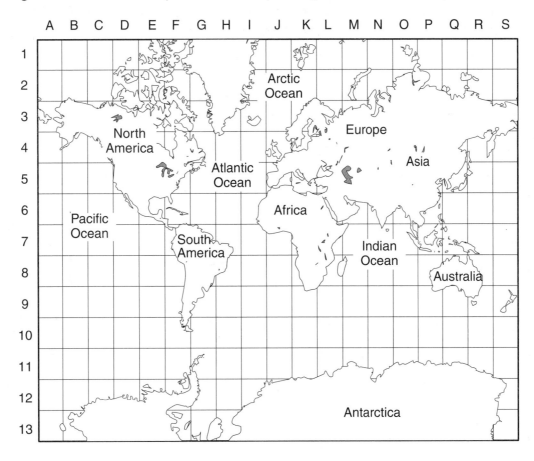

1. What continent is located at 3R?

   _____

2. What continent is located at 8G?

   _____

3. If you were at 5I, would you be in a car or in a boat?

   _____

4. What ocean is located at 8B?

   _____

5. What continent would you find at 8K?

   _____

6. What continent would find at 8Q?

   _____

Globes

The earth is round, not flat. Even though flat maps can show different parts of our planet, a globe gives us a truer picture of what Earth is really like. A globe is a model of Earth. It is round like Earth and can rotate like Earth rotates.

Color the water blue and the land green. Then answer the questions below.

1. What continents can be seen in their entirety on the globe above?

   _____

2. What would you need to do in order to see Asia, Europe, and Africa?

   _____

3. Which is more like Earth, a flat map or a globe? _____

   Why? _____

   _____

Divided up into Hemispheres

Earth is divided into two parts by an imaginary line. This line is called the equator. The part of Earth that is above the line is called the Northern Hemisphere. The part that is below the line is the Southern Hemisphere.

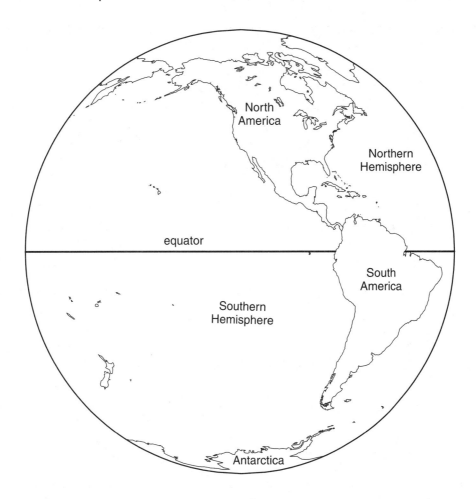

1. Trace the equator using a red crayon.

2. Draw a star on the Northern Hemisphere.

3. Draw a check mark on the Southern Hemisphere.

4. What continent on this map is completely in the Northern Hemisphere?

   _____

5. What two continents on this map are in the Southern Hemisphere?

   _____

6. The equator passes through what continent on this map?

   _____

Even More Hemispheres

Earth is divided into Northern and Southern Hemispheres. It is also divided in another way. An imaginary line separates the east side from the west side. These are the Eastern and Western Hemispheres. Use the two halves of a globe below to answer the questions.

1. North America is in which two hemispheres?

   _____

2. South America is in which three hemispheres?

   _____

3. What other continents can be found in three hemispheres?

   _____

4. Is Australia in the Western Hemisphere?

   _____

5. Which continents are in the Northern Hemisphere? (Hint: Use both pictures to help you.)

   _____

6. The equator passes through which continents?

   _____

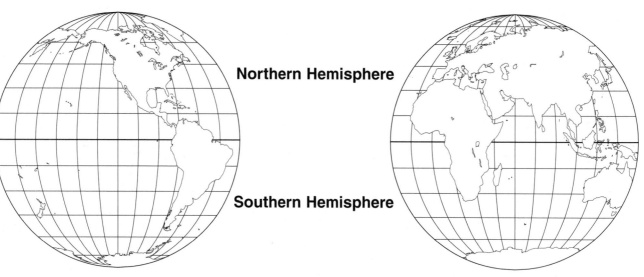

Arctic Circle

The Arctic Circle is at the top of the Northern Hemisphere. You can see on the map below that the North Pole is in the middle of the Arctic Ocean. Parts of many countries are located within the Arctic Circle. These places are very, very cold.

This map shows countries, islands, an ocean, and smaller bodies of water. The country names are in capital letters.

Use the map of the Arctic Circle to answer the questions on page 34.

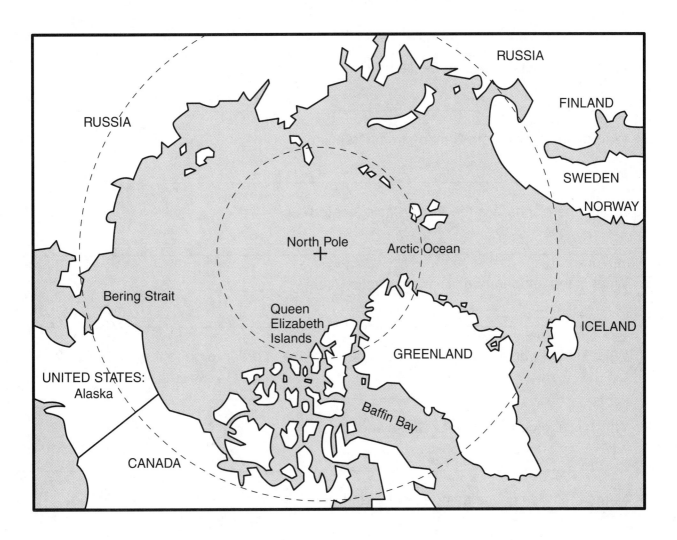

Arctic Circle *(cont.)*

Use the map of the Arctic Circle and the information on page 33 to answer the questions below.

1. Which country borders Alaska?

   _____

2. What stretch of water separates Alaska from Russia?

   _____

3. Which country is closest to the North Pole?

   _____

4. Which islands separate Canada from Greenland?

   _____

5. In what hemisphere is the Arctic Circle located?

   _____

6. What is the temperature like in the Arctic Circle?

   _____

7. What kind of transportation would you need to use in order to go to the North Pole?

   _____

8. Which island country is near Greenland?

   _____

9. Name the three countries north of Iceland.

   _____

10. What is the name of the bay near Greenland?

    _____

Product Maps

Some maps are used to show the kinds of things that are grown, raised, or made in a certain place. For example, a map could show that a place is known for farming or raising cattle. This kind of map is called a product map. Look at the product map below for the state of Michigan. You can see that there are many products that are grown and raised there. Use the map to answer the questions below. (**Note:** This map does not indicate all products grown, raised, or made in Michigan.)

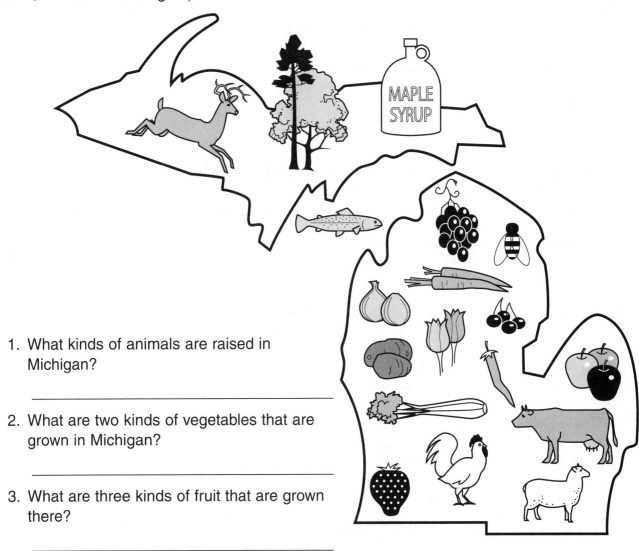

1. What kinds of animals are raised in Michigan?

   _____

2. What are two kinds of vegetables that are grown in Michigan?

   _____

3. What are three kinds of fruit that are grown there?

   _____

4. What do you think the flowers represent?

   _____

5. What three animals on this map would most likely live on a farm?

   _____

6. What do you think the bee on this map represents?

   _____

Make Your Own Product Map

Create your own imaginary state. Draw a symbol to represent each product listed in the key. You can even create three more products. Remember that products can also include things that are taken from the earth, such as oil, minerals, or trees. Products can also include things that are made, such as clothes. Use your imagination and draw the products on the map of your state.

Name of State: _____

Product Key

_____ _____ _____

_____ _____ _____

Weather Maps

There are many kinds of weather maps. Some show where it is sunny, rainy, cloudy, and snowy. Some show the high or low temperatures. Some weather maps even show where there are lightning strikes or even where pollen affects people's health.

Use the map below of the western United States to answer the questions.

1. Which states will have sun and no rain? _____

2. Which states will be partly cloudy? _____

3. Which states will have two kinds of weather? _____

4. What will the weather be like in Oregon?_____

5. What will the weather be like in Utah? _____

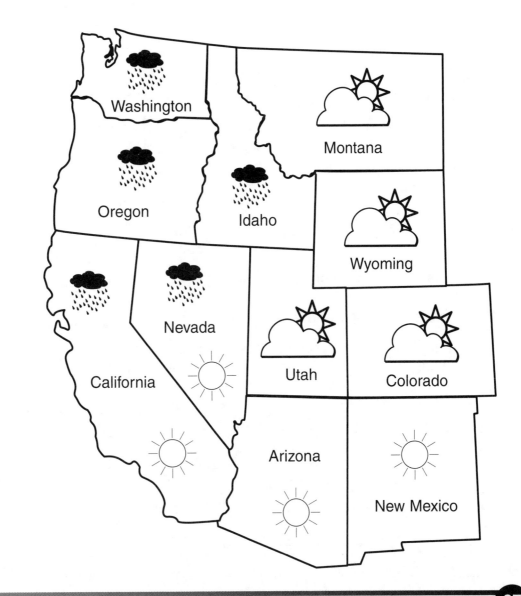

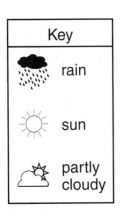

More Weather Maps

Here is another map of the Western United States. This map shows the temperatures during the early winter months.

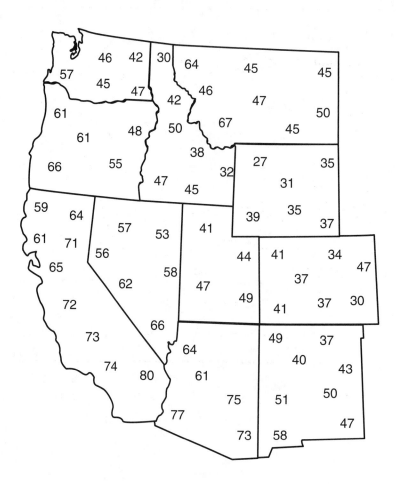

1. Which state shows the coldest temperature? _____

2. Which state shows the warmest temperature? _____

3. Look at the temperatures on the coast. How are they different from the ones that are farther inland?

   _____

4. Some places have temperatures in the 70s and 80s. Are these places in the North or the South?

   _____

5. Which two states have temperatures in the 70's and higher?

   _____

Use the compass rose and key to answer the questions.

Pine Grove

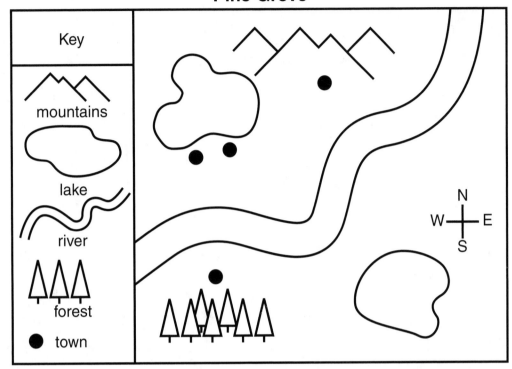

1. The mountains are in the
   - (A) south.
   - (B) east.
   - (C) west.
   - (D) north.

2. The forest is in which part of Pine Grove?
   - (A) northeast
   - (B) northwest
   - (C) southeast
   - (D) southwest

3. What is in the southeast part of the map?
   - (A) town
   - (B) lake
   - (C) mountains
   - (D) forest

4. Two towns are beside a
   - (A) mountain.
   - (B) lake.
   - (C) river.
   - (D) forest.

5. If you were in the mountains, in which direction would you travel to get to the forest?
   - (A) southwest
   - (B) south
   - (C) southeast
   - (D) north

6. What separates the two lakes?
   - (A) a river
   - (B) mountains
   - (C) two towns
   - (D) a forest

Practice Test 2

Use the scale to answer the questions about the map.

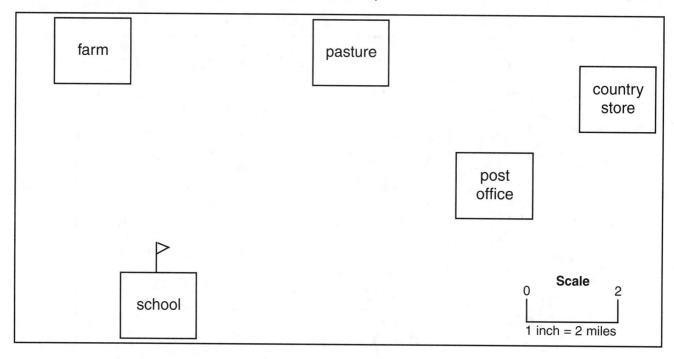

farm

pasture

country store

post office

school

Scale

0   2

1 inch = 2 miles

1. On the scale, an inch equals
   - (A) 2 kilometers.
   - (B) 1 mile.
   - (C) 2 miles.
   - (D) 5 miles.

2. How many miles apart are the farm and the country store?
   - (A) about 4 miles
   - (B) about 10 miles
   - (C) about 6 miles
   - (D) about 12 miles

3. How many miles apart are the school and the country store?
   - (A) about 12 miles
   - (B) about 5 miles
   - (C) about 2 miles
   - (D) about 8 miles

4. How many miles apart are the country store and the post office?
   - (A) about 2 miles
   - (B) about 1 mile
   - (C) about 4 miles
   - (D) about 3 miles

5. How many miles is it from the farm to the pasture?
   - (A) about 2 miles
   - (B) about 4 miles
   - (C) about 3 miles
   - (D) about 5 miles

6. If you were at the farm and drove to the pasture and then to the school, how many miles would it be?
   - (A) about 9 miles
   - (B) about 15 miles
   - (C) about 11 miles
   - (D) about 12 miles

Practice Test 3

Use the milage chart to answer the questions below.

	Detroit, MI	Portland, OR	Toledo, OH	Wichita, KS
Boise, ID	1,942	432	1,908	1,312
Madison, WI	406	1,950	372	676
Phoenix, AZ	1,957	1,266	1,901	1,025
Omaha, NE	716	1,654	681	298

1. How far apart are Madison and Toledo?
   A) 1,942 miles
   B) 676 miles
   C) 372 miles
   D) 406 miles

2. How many miles apart are Omaha and Wichita?
   A) 716 miles
   B) 372 miles
   C) 1,950 miles
   D) 298 miles

3. Which city on the chart is closest to Boise?
   A) Wichita
   B) Toledo
   C) Portland
   D) Detroit

4. Which city on the chart is farthest away from Detroit?
   A) Phoenix
   B) Omaha
   C) Madison
   D) Boise

5. Which city on the chart is closest to Portland?
   A) Madison
   B) Boise
   C) Omaha
   D) Phoenix

6. How many miles apart are Phoenix and Detroit?
   A) 372 miles
   B) 1,942 miles
   C) 1,266 miles
   D) 1,957 miles

Practice Test 4

Use the map and grid to answer the questions.

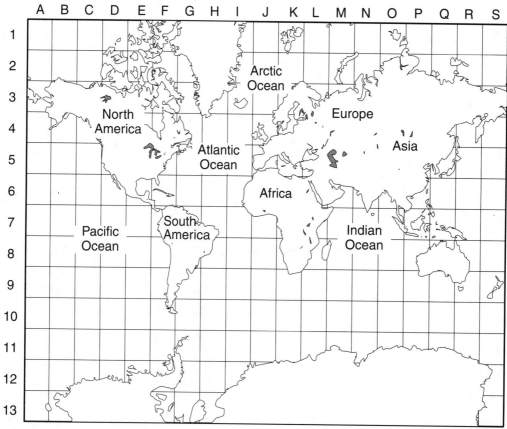

1. What is located at 3J?

   (A) Atlantic Ocean

   (B) North America

   (C) Arctic Ocean

   (D) Africa

2. What ocean is located at 11D?

   (A) Pacific Ocean

   (B) South America

   (C) Asia

   (D) Indian Ocean

3. 3B and 5D are both a part of what?

   (A) North America

   (B) Atlantic Ocean

   (C) Europe

   (D) Asia

4. What ocean is south of 4N?

   (A) Indian Ocean

   (B) Pacific Ocean

   (C) Atlantic Ocean

   (D) both the Atlantic and Pacific Oceans

5. Which of the coordinates below is completey in water?

   (A) 3K

   (B) 9O

   (C) 3P

   (D) 12L

6. Which of the coordinates below is in an ocean?

   (A) 2H   (C) 5E

   (B) 6K   (D) 5H

Practice Test 5

Answer the questions about the hemispheres.

Western Hemisphere

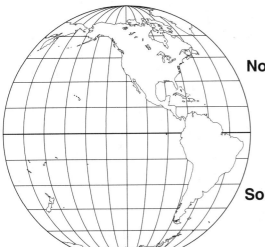

Eastern Hemisphere

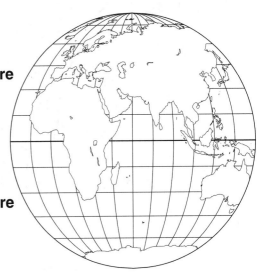

Northern Hemisphere

Southern Hemisphere

1. North America is in which two hemispheres?

   Ⓐ Eastern and Western

   Ⓑ Northern and Western

   Ⓒ Northern and Eastern

   Ⓓ Southern and Eastern

2. Asia is in which two hemispheres?

   Ⓐ Southern and Eastern

   Ⓑ Southern and Western

   Ⓒ Northern and Western

   Ⓓ Northern and Eastern

3. Australia is in which two hemispheres?

   Ⓐ Northern and Eastern

   Ⓑ Western and Southern

   Ⓒ Southern and Eastern

   Ⓓ Western and Northern

4. Which continent is completely within the Northern Hemisphere?

   Ⓐ South America

   Ⓑ Antarctica

   Ⓒ Europe

   Ⓓ Australia

5. Which two continents are in both the Northern and Southern Hemispheres?

   Ⓐ Europe and Asia

   Ⓑ South America and Africa

   Ⓒ South America and Antarctica

   Ⓓ North America and Asia

6. In which two hemispheres is Canada located?

   Ⓐ Northern and Western

   Ⓑ Northern and Eastern

   Ⓒ Southern and Western

   Ⓓ Southern and Eastern

Practice Test 6

Use the map to answer the questions.

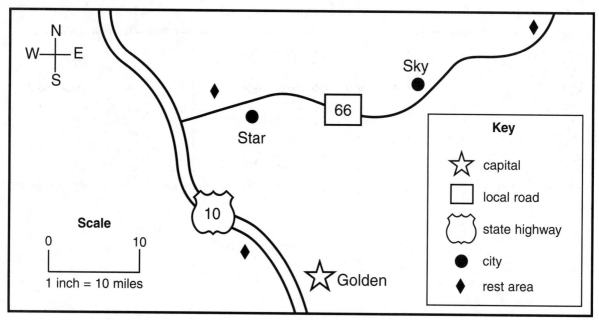

1. What does the diamond represent on the map?

    (A) a city

    (B) the capital city

    (C) a rest area

    (D) a highway

2. How many miles is it from Star to Sky?

    (A) 2 miles

    (B) 4 miles

    (C) 10 miles

    (D) 20 miles

3. The capital city is near what kind of road?

    (A) a local road

    (B) a dirt road

    (C) a small road

    (D) a state highway

4. Using highway 66 and road 10, how many miles is it from Sky to Golden?

    (A) 5 miles

    (B) 10 miles

    (C) 25 miles

    (D) 50 miles

5. How many rest areas are on the local road?

    (A) two

    (B) one

    (C) three

    (D) five

6. In which direction does road 10 run?

    (A) East

    (B) Southeast

    (C) West

    (D) Southwest

Answer Sheet

Test Practice 1	Test Practice 2	Test Practice 3
1. Ⓐ Ⓑ Ⓒ Ⓓ	1. Ⓐ Ⓑ Ⓒ Ⓓ	1. Ⓐ Ⓑ Ⓒ Ⓓ
2. Ⓐ Ⓑ Ⓒ Ⓓ	2. Ⓐ Ⓑ Ⓒ Ⓓ	2. Ⓐ Ⓑ Ⓒ Ⓓ
3. Ⓐ Ⓑ Ⓒ Ⓓ	3. Ⓐ Ⓑ Ⓒ Ⓓ	3. Ⓐ Ⓑ Ⓒ Ⓓ
4. Ⓐ Ⓑ Ⓒ Ⓓ	4. Ⓐ Ⓑ Ⓒ Ⓓ	4. Ⓐ Ⓑ Ⓒ Ⓓ
5. Ⓐ Ⓑ Ⓒ Ⓓ	5. Ⓐ Ⓑ Ⓒ Ⓓ	5. Ⓐ Ⓑ Ⓒ Ⓓ
6. Ⓐ Ⓑ Ⓒ Ⓓ	6. Ⓐ Ⓑ Ⓒ Ⓓ	6. Ⓐ Ⓑ Ⓒ Ⓓ

Test Practice 4	Test Practice 5	Test Practice 6
1. Ⓐ Ⓑ Ⓒ Ⓓ	1. Ⓐ Ⓑ Ⓒ Ⓓ	1. Ⓐ Ⓑ Ⓒ Ⓓ
2. Ⓐ Ⓑ Ⓒ Ⓓ	2. Ⓐ Ⓑ Ⓒ Ⓓ	2. Ⓐ Ⓑ Ⓒ Ⓓ
3. Ⓐ Ⓑ Ⓒ Ⓓ	3. Ⓐ Ⓑ Ⓒ Ⓓ	3. Ⓐ Ⓑ Ⓒ Ⓓ
4. Ⓐ Ⓑ Ⓒ Ⓓ	4. Ⓐ Ⓑ Ⓒ Ⓓ	4. Ⓐ Ⓑ Ⓒ Ⓓ
5. Ⓐ Ⓑ Ⓒ Ⓓ	5. Ⓐ Ⓑ Ⓒ Ⓓ	5. Ⓐ Ⓑ Ⓒ Ⓓ
6. Ⓐ Ⓑ Ⓒ Ⓓ	6. Ⓐ Ⓑ Ⓒ Ⓓ	6. Ⓐ Ⓑ Ⓒ Ⓓ

Answer Key

Page 4
1. a place
2. any three of the following: world, country, state, city, weather, population
3. any two of the following: streets, highways, schools, attractions, landmarks
4. It is round and turns.
5. Earth
6. information about places

Page 5
1. South
2. North
3. East
4. West, East
5. North, South
6. West, East, South

Page 6
1. NW
2. SW
3. NE
4. SE
5. NW, SW
6. NW, SW, NE, SE

Page 7
1. Pine Road
2. Second Street
3. Ice Cream Shop
4. Movie Theater
5. Southeast
6. Ice Cream Shop and Fast Food Restaurant

Page 9
1. Shady Park
2. North/South
3. Park Lake
4. Southeast
5. East or Southeast
6. West

7. Highways 2 and 3
8. northeast
9. southeast
10. Green Park

Page 10
1. true
2. false; western and southeastern
3. false; northeast
4. false; only one, the others are reached by local roads
5. true
6. true
7. false; west of lake, east of railroad
8. true

Page 11
1. school
2. picnic area, library, and playground
3. the library
4. southeast
5. eight
6. northeast

Page 13
1. the capital city
2. cities
3. a lake
4. Tallahassee
5. Lake Okeechobee
6. Jacksonville
7. a national park
8. Atlantic Ocean
9. Lake Okeechobee
10. Southwest

Page 17
1. any three of the following: Plymouth, Bristol, Portsmouth, Dover, London,
2. Birmingham
3. north
4. the capital city

Answer Key (cont.)

5. cities
6. London
7. northwest
8. the Irish Sea
9. Thames
10. Thames

Page 18

1. 1 mile
2. 2 miles
3. 1½ inches
4. 1½ miles
5. 4 miles
6. 1 mile
7. 3 miles

Page 19

1. 3 miles
2. 4 miles
3. 5 miles
4. 5 miles
5. 5 miles
6. 6 miles

Page 21

1. about 450 miles (750 km)
2. about 150 miles (300 km)
3. Wood Buffalo National Park
4. about 150 miles (300 km)
5. about 300 miles (a little more than 500 km)
6. about 187 miles (a little more than 325 km)
7. It is farther to go from Edmonton to Medicine Hat.
8. about 300 miles (a little more than 500 km)
9. about 200 km
10. about 487 miles

Page 23

1. 1,949 miles
2. 401 miles
3. Norfolk

4. Denver
5. Tulsa and Dallas
6. Norfolk and Los Angeles
7. about five hours
8. about nine hours
9. Boston
10. Miami

Page 24

1. Answers will vary.
2. Atlantic Ocean and Indian Ocean
3. Indian Ocean
4. North America and South America
5. Atlantic Ocean
6. South America

Page 26

1. New Mexico, Oklahoma, Arkansas, Louisiana
2. any three of the following: Alabama, Alaska, Arizona, Arkansas
3. Kansas, Colorado, Wyoming, South Dakota, Iowa, Missouri

Page 27

1. three
2. Edmonton or Calgary
3. Nunavut, Manitoba, Ontario, Quebec
4. Ottawa or Toronto
5. Lake Superior, Lake Michigan, Lake Huron, Lake Ontario, and Lake Erie
6. the Northwest Territory

Page 29

1. Asia
2. South America
3. boat
4. Pacific Ocean
5. Africa
6. Australia

Answer Key (cont.)

Page 30
1. North America and South America
2. turn the globe to the other side
3. A globe is more like Earth because it is round and it rotates.

Page 31
4. North America
5. South America and Antarctica
6. South America

Page 32
1. Northern and Western
2. Northern, Southern, and Western
3. Antarctica, Africa, Asia
4. no
5. North America, Africa, Europe, Asia
6. South America, Africa

Page 34
1. Canada
2. the Bering Strait
3. Greenland
4. the Queen Elizabeth Islands
5. the Northern Hemisphere
6. very cold
7. a boat
8. Iceland
9. Finland, Sweden, and Norway
10. Baffin Bay

Page 35
1. cows, chickens, sheep
2. any two, such as onions, celery, carrots, tomatoes, potatoes
3. any three, such as apples, grapes, strawberries, cherries
4. growing and selling flowers
5. cows, chickens, sheep
6. honey production

Page 37
1. Arizona and New Mexico
2. Montana, Wyoming, Utah, and Colorado
3. California and Nevada
4. rainy
5. partly cloudy

Page 38
1. Wyoming
2. California
3. The temperatures are cooler near the coast.
4. in the south
5. Arizona and California

Pages 39
1. D
2. D
3. B
4. B
5. A
6. A

Pages 40
1. C
2. B
3. D
4. B
5. B
6. A

Pages 41
1. C
2. D
3. C
4. A
5. B
6. D

Pages 42
1. C
2. A
3. A
4. A
5. B
6. D

Pages 43
1. B
2. D
3. C
4. C
5. B
6. A

Pages 44
1. C
2. D
3. A
4. D
5. B
6. B